"In this astonishing achievement of a book, Charity Yoro expands the artistic repertoire of poetry with refreshing self-awareness, technical dexterity, and grace. Whether working in inherited forms, found forms, or invented ones, ***Yoro's writing is marked by a singularity of voice and vision. She is clearly a rising star in the contemporary literary landscape.***"

—KRISTINA MARIE DARLING
AUTHOR OF *DAYLIGHT HAS ALREADY COME*
& X MARKS THE DRESS: A REGISTRY

"Fifty years ago the Hawaiʻian activist and comedian Kehau Lee Jackson said, 'Our country is being plasticized, cheapened, and exploited.' Charity Yoro's piquant, gorgeous first collection, *ten-cent flower & other territories*, documents the personal and social toll of this continuing disenfranchisement, as it hauntingly delineates vistas and cityscapes from Bangkok to Hawaiʻi and the U.S. mainland. ***'Fractal, webbed,' Yoro's intricate and inventive poems flash with memorable phrasings, imagining into being a 'territory of unmastered language.'*** It's not a book for tourists. Readers who attend closely to its 'sunken moon prayers,' though, will find a new voice of rare insight, commitment, and beauty."

—JOHN BEER
AUTHOR OF *THE WASTE LAND AND OTHER POEMS*

FIRSTMATTERPRESS

Portland, Ore.

ten-cent flower
& other territories

ten-cent flower
& other territories

charity e. yoro

FIRSTMATTERPRESS
Portland, Ore.

First Edition

Published in the United States
by First Matter Press
Portland, Oregon

Paperback ISBN-13: 978-1-958600-05-4
Library of Congress Control Number: 2023943357

Regional Arts & Culture Council

This literary arts project was funded by Regional Arts
and Culture Council's Arts3C Grant Program for
Creation, Cultivation & Community in the Portland
metropolitan tri-county region. www.racc.org

Editor: Lauren Paredes
Contributing Editors: ash good & Emily Moon
In Cohort: Rae Diamond
Contributing Readers: Hailey Spencer & Jessica E. Pierce
Copy Editor: Andra Vltavín

Cover Illustration
Copyright © 2023 by Lara Rouse
@good_luck_lara

Book design by ash good
ashgood.com

for roya & noemi,
my two favorite poems

poems

I : coda

There is no life outside empire. All paradise is performance
for people who pay. Perhaps I'm an invader and feel I haven't paid.
—Brenda Shaughnessy

I want to root a
garden into a home while also
being carried out by the current.
These are contradictions we
want to find essential, to say,
moon, here I come.
—Jennifer S. Cheng

I am remembering, and I am writing a poem in my many tongues.
—Camille T. Dungy

inherit the wind

for p ʻda hau and waimānalo

this wild coastal grass and lady steelhead sojourn
is the windsound i cup my ear against / the song
of chipped seashorn trumpet / the call to return
home / i hear / the hollow / my heel over throng
of bush & bee / snare in this unkempt symphony
/ territory of unmastered language / brash birdcall
above head / how these warbled trees unnaturally
bend / as mother trout treads upstream / so small
our worlds / rivers and shores / we ʻre not home
to defend / save the fine rare grains / wooded memory
from extraction / each flattened parceled foamed
wave stands defiant / the island ʻs last eastside beach
/ a wonder how she returns / to birth at the mouth
of the river / whose new name she can ʻt pronounce

our lady of 'iolani

DOWN

1 _____ islands in the Hawaiian archipelago, not one of them named Waikiki

2 Shipwreck, now a monument, USS _____

5 The apostrophe that is not an apostrophe that like so many words, the hundreds of names for wind, does not translate well

6 What tourism feels like to a local

7 The only royal palace on US soil

8 Maunakea, home of the largest telescope in the Northern _____

9 Naval airfield on the bay, home to the best breaks on the eastside, where the boys run from MP, get caught stealing sunset swells

10 The person who appears first when you Google "Hawaiian monuments:" Captain _____ ____ (two words)

12 [See 19 across] The morality of the act committed against Queen Liliuʻokalani and the Kānaka Maoli. As in _____ house arrest. As in stolen lands, also _____

ACROSS

3 Surpasses sugar and pineapple as the dominant driver of the Hawaiian economy

4 [See 10 down] He was not, in fact, ____, fertility god

8 Donʻt let its soft pronunciation fool you; this is no paradise

9 Responsibility, yours and mine

11 Leprosy, exile

13 What tourism feels like to Hawaiʻi

14 Aliʻi, or the _____ class

15 [See 10 down] He brought the gift of

    _____

16 What Hawaiʻi feels like to a tourist

17 Pearl _____

18 Offshore landowners

19 The practice of greeting and welcoming, Hawaiian hospitality (how the kingdom was overthrown). With a honihoni on the cheek, slippas at the door, an invitation to stay, but not too long, bumbai we get sent to live at the California Hotel on the ninth isle

The *'okina* in *Hawai'i* is often misspelled, replaced with an easier
punctuation. Or *tourism*. Speaking of *displacement,* don't you hate how
Lono autocorrects to "long," as if the erasure of another deity is
necessary, *illegal* body navigating the unclaimed pacific *hemisphere* by
star, naked eye. Our streets are named after *thieves.* Start with *Kāne'ohe.*
Start with *James Cook,* who centuries later, a dying language thanks for
syphilis. Now, when someone, without asking, tells me about their
expensive vacation on my home island, explains that it was their "least
favorite" of the *eight,* goes on to say how they'd rather spend
Christmas in Mexico next year, I want to ask, as members of the *ruling*
class, bearers of this postcolonial currency (passport stamps), you
must know *ho'okipa.* That the world is an island. That this particular
island is a *harbor* of matters unsettled, perfectly positioned to settle all
four branches of the U.S. military. Territory of the land of the free of
rape charges. I want to say, before you leave to spend the rest of the
year back in *Arizona* or Ontario, please pay respects at *'Iolani* Palace,
learn about *Kalaupapa,* understand your *kuleana.* Instead, I warn you
not to leave with lava rock in your luggage.

sugar in the raw

great grandma—what
was your name?
we've lost   our kos-
eki somewhere   along
the way   no photo
no   altar
i   empty
the sweet   the queen's
ōhiʻa lehua hidden
in the morning paper

outer-island layover

i take a picture
      of the frothing
at my toes:

          a snapshot

of choosing
      to land   as simple as

to stand
        as natural as
    salt on sun-
       freckled skin:
         mom & i

walk down
    the shore
parceled by
    mainland
       chain hotels
   —i wonder
      if the order
   is alphabetical

dinner is over
    salted & inter
       rupted by a

                    performance
          that feels ex
                    ploitative

          the girl looks too
                    young, keeps pulling
                              at her pa'u skirt while
          the braddah on his pū
                    is short on breath, no
          mo *ha* in aloha

meanwhile the aunty
          at the prime ocean
front property next
                    door teaches the haole
          how to umi

does it ever get old?
          teaching them, i mean

mom asks about
          my feelings on
                    tiki torches
(she likes them)

i don't want
          to get into it

          so i refrain
      from saying
          out loud
     what she
already knows:

     no fucking
         way i'm getting
             married on
     the beach.

hoku

my dreams write through me

poems i feel small against

sunken moon prayers

hurricane

the baby pretzels are furikake-laced, shiny with butter, everything
unpronounceable, blended with corn, honeycomb & bugle. what was
once a luxury is now comfort dished in a tiny white ramekin on our
dinner table. before spam musubi, there was vienna sausage &
a microwave. smashed saimin straight from the bag, MSG sucked
from a tiny foil packet, the yellow stain of artificial chicken on our skin.
they warned we'd grow worms the shape of curly dehydrated noodles
in our bellies. big boddah fo' boil waddah but. us kids, with our eyes-
bigger-than-our-opu. scrambled eggs for supper sometimes, but
always full full full to the tin. at a mainland bar someday soon, i'll find
a grain-free version of hurricane chex next to my $13 cocktail.
small kid time in a rose gold-plated vessel.

lanikai

your fineness sticks to every sea-soaked
surface, every crevice, to towel frays
& toenails & the condensation on plastic
containers of tako poke & salsa from safeway

even a good rinse
can't rid you
from naked skin
flavoring each bite
of dipped corn chip

in the laundry next sunday, i will find
grains of you ground to pure white, life
times of grating wave & coral stem
& broken glass

find you in the bottom
of jean skirt pockets
hold you to my nostrils
& breathe you in, taste what
it means to be invincible

parcel

ownership: the state   the land

in the state's hands   air force   after the land

the military   the state   lands

conservation   improvements

     perimeter   fencing   picnicking   camping

comfort   landscaping   a caretaker's house   the park

     the city   renamed   responsibility   wealth

resources   views   access   picturesque

stands ironwood   large   open   spaces

known   sites   active   engaged   community

the foundation: the aging
facilities essential
time   coastal
taken   toll
states   disrepair

leaking broken
graffiti design
rehabilitation

suffered the elements / habitable
space / deteriorating in the absence
parked residence / highly visible
visitor   little function

disposal the base
                unused
recreation   overgrown
        thick tangle
introduced vegetation   dominated by haole

a more perfect union (misplaced accent)

wē he *people* o hē un i e a
ʻīo e ō o m a mo e pe e *union*
e a lih u i e in u e ome i an uili
p o i e o he ommon e en e p omo e
he ene al wel a e an e u e he le in
o *lie* o ou el e an ou po e i o
o ain an e a li h i on i u ion o he
uni e aʻe o ame i a

to sift grave scrape
divide the line between
lands say supreme
stingy prolonged sound
or thing chanting drawn
out wail of superior air
answer: resonance
remain endure survive
exist   journey
native trees   northeast wind
contiguous adjoining
next approaching

act of math

for haunani-kay trask

you learn *discovery*
+ *resolution*
before you learn
venereal   safe sex
is not a footnote
      in the scripture

+ the delineations of ~~mainland~~ states
        + to sing his praises, most high:
            god is   good
            god is   bountiful
            god is   not earth(ly possessions)
            god is   not water—loose, like your women

        find ola hou in JESUS
              here is your free condom (1)
                pocket KJV bible (1)

+ your acres (3)   for 10% of you   of the one-third saved
     from sailor's gifts   the everlasting gift saved by the precious
                blood
                of JESUS, amene!

                may *the lord's will* be done
                in the islands as it is
                on the continent

you learn percentages: *blood quantum,*
the privatization of rain, how to parcel
ahupuaʻa like gutting a fish:

      suck your lipskin raw
            on the sweet green stalk   harvested by settlers
                          on the iwi
                              of your ancestors

   the great māhele divides more than   the land

      today, god is an algorithm
          you know your arithmetic

très passing: a series

*

he asks you what you're looking for
as you squint, pretend intent, searching
for something   that doesn't exist
between the jersey sheets   still sticky
from the excessive plastic packaging
          and him, your honeyed spoon

you tell him without pause, without
wanting to go deep or at least
philosophical at 4 in the morning:

i'm looking for a reason

you laugh together   he calls you
          his poet

pulls you
back
into the
folds—
tenderly,
the ring
stings
your
cheek

& you can't
        fall back
asleep,   not for
        just
                five
        minutes
                        more

*

a heavy bass line. predictable, strong. the heartbeat. a softness,
surprising, mounts: mournful strings. violin or slow plucking of harp.

the notes, a series
of snapshots, sweet
repetitive goodbyes

song ends
               on the color   *blush*

                                   sounds

the current parting
        the gauzy rose curtains where

                your other self floats before
                   tiptoeing back upstairs
                               your flushed, freshly
          fucked cheeks, a color that rings in your ears for days on
    end
            the rare dusk that opens
                for you, the spectrum of sense
available, waiting

        the chilled wine you have yet

          to permit yourselves to sip

* *in the southern hemisphere, constellations are reversed* ★

★

aloha
or how
many ways
you have learned
to say   goodbye: you knew
you would leave   the continent
no one could find   on a map
without a note   because you could not
face why you   were no better than
the french miners   raping
the highlands with their hungry
machines   scarring sacred stone
you too   dishonored   the body
rubbing leaves violently between
forefinger & thumb to capture
the fragrance of eucalyptus
using *veloma* & *salamooooooh*
& bags of undocumented cloves
as cheap party tricks   even now
crossing austra-indo-pacific seas
in dreams   returning to find
fluency without consent
....

*_*_*_*

om shala mala beads
seven white women
three rows of seats &
one precarious parallel
parking spot [cue clapping]

zen den goddess lair but
not a harem *how offensive*
cumin ghee chia seeds
gut health nepalese
prayer flag flapping anti-

inflammatory remedy
recipe exchange man-
dala womb crystalline
sound bath meditating
singing bowls burning

greenhouse gases *oh GOD-
DESS* the gardener using
roundup on the dairy
gluten substance free
range certified organic

divine! abundance!
blessings! sing doctor
lawyer analyst
real estate agent
activist vice president

have you heard of
resistant starch, not
a diet, a *lifestyle change*
but i'm so full i can't
eat another bite

i'm trying to gain
weight actually, you
first, i insist, i don't
eat in the morning
i don't eat

at night, let's go on
a hike, do yoga to
deserve our meals
doesn't that feel
great? eat MORE

your ethnic-chic accent
pillows from new renaissance
your hired acupuncturist slash
astrologist your fucking winter
beach house in hawaiʻi

more please & blessings

opus on verdigris

too obvious   to call it   brassy   doesn't capture   the complexity

force nor fragility   of ivory   key parts   you hear   its acidity

stinging   raw parts   of gum   & side-tongue   sores   curling

olive pits &   plum vinegar   feta cheese   between cheek-skin

you first experienced it at six or seven as the third wheel on your mother's *real* date with some haole guy from church probably military kenny g at the blaisdell & the man with his sax took the hana hou too literally & you & mom were both falling asleep & eyeing each other like *let's go already* no more encore but the date was our ride & he kept clapping *clueless* that bar

off kapiolani   behind femme nu

the strip club

where everyone

had a high   school friend

dancing   to put themselves   thru community   college

jazzminds   with its   mis-

matched plush   love seats

shared

couches   neon   blinking

bouncer   from the westside   who went elementary   w/

your calabash   cousin's   best   friend

side-nodded   you in   all the time   with your   real cousin's

expired ID   picture   of shorter   lighter version

you

a more   pronounced   nose

you just had   to remember   not to smile   when you

    ordered your   glass of merlot   like in the movies

like you don't   care

    having found   your place

    sitting alone

ambient abecedarian

acerbic anemone bearing chimera caesura
destiny ecclesiastic elegance fawn graceless
gloam hour interstitial home jeweled
kindred mollusk legacy mercy never own
provenant pastoral porous periphery query
roam sable seam tenor tilted-plane undulate
volta waxing yesterday's poetic zenith

ten-cent flower

in bangkok, i use the back of my hand
to extract a sooty, sticky drip from my nose

—the smell of home: *puakenikeni.*
here, the fragile white flowers grace

shrines the size of birdhouses, next to
bowls of rice & deferential fruit flies &

icy rust-stained bottles of orange fanta.
at home, the sap sticks to children's fingers,

fruit plucked too young from low-hanging
branches, gathered in plastic foodland bags

& strung into congratulatory strands: birthdays,
graduations, just-cuz-aloha-fridays... sweet

stems assaulting saccharine lingering long
after the life of the party. i've sung my lineage

for those confused about my *exact* origins
needing to *place* & *order* & *root* me

before enjoying me, carefully curated cut of
meat, while our families make house

on the ninth island, at the edges of deserts,
flashing neon & slot machines: the only place

we can live like the kings & queens
of a monarchy that was never ours.

my house is a museum of pretty
stolen things, lei placed delicately

on bare burnt shoulders, obligatory
kiss on cheek, a taste of paradise

that has never belonged to me, either.

māhealani

my cousin taught me

the word for full is never
with his sharp-horned tongue

[+]

houseguest

i'll tell you how it ends
this story of crumpled sheets
cold toes drawing circles
—a sumi-e landscape

the way it begins: running
lover to lover, a number, a knock,
spilled ink, staining, arranging
shapes on a page

false alarm[1]

I.   8:07 a.m.

she sleeps with fear
            under her pillow
in the shape of a hand
            gun, magazine
locked & loaded
            queen mattress
only she over-
            turns to access.
it's nyquil sometimes
            wine or CBD
melatonin or trazodone
            restless nonetheless
through the night
            a child's sound
machine drowning
            her anxieties
her church screams
            things
speaks in tongues
            while she tells me
the assets are in my name
            should anything
happen

[1] ~~On the morning of~~ Too early on Saturday, January 13, 2018, a ~~ballistic missile alert was accidentally~~ false alarm was issued via the Emergency Alert System and Wireless Emergency Alert System ~~over television, radio, and cellphones~~ as a pop-up appearing below Trump's latest tweet in the ~~U.S. state~~ occupied territory of ~~Hawaii~~ Hawai'i. BALLISTIC MISSILE THREAT INBOUND TO HAWAII. SEEK IMMEDIATE SHELTER. THIS IS NOT A DRILL. became the subject of many viral memes.

II.   *Sequence of the End of Days*

the assets are

in the shape of a hand

restless nonetheless

in tongues

sometimes

locked & loaded

screams

through the night

a child's sound

drowning

fear

under her pillow

sublimity, OR

a tour of boneyard once-homes   incinerated
skeletal frames where only brick hearths remain
& bright blue flags lay claim like conquests or
declarations of defiance
                            WE WILL REBUILD

we have lost seconds of breath   tense
through rippling stars to the exit signaling we're in
bitter, wintry pine country:

              the door's unlocked, but the cross out front

                    tongues
                              threats
                                    flames

              lost   once
        declarations   *go home*
                  cross   country

we have lost

                    breath
          stars   exiting   the baby's wail

rules of negotiation

That they argue over the shade of shelled pistachio, which he says is the same as the name of the tea that tastes faintly of barley. And that while they are on the subject, she says, mustard greens taste sweet. That, in one lifetime, an oyster was a peace offering. That it's the season of dying but they'd never know it, bears shortening their years by hours of lost sleep. That they drove three hours in the rain to sit in a hot tub in a hailstorm. That they walk through the whiteness, bare ass, hand in hand. That she's always hungry, or cold. That when she drinks, the wine warms. But when she sees herself, crimson lips & stained teeth, reflected she realizes she likes everyone else more. That the skin and the shell and the meat are separate things. That she cried when she came and couldn't say why, pulled him closer until she could pull herself together, until he said: I felt that. That all she wants is to slide into his runner sweats and lay between the carpet of his thighs. That all she wants is a home shaped like a letter she learned once—not the first, but the most significant sound. That despite herself, she lifts her arm as if to swim across the bank of snow. That she forgets most times her gestures don't translate here. That the navigation will lie. That the flurries will melt wet. That the tires are afraid of losing what they think they have captured between their creases. That love is, sometimes, traction.

That the passage through suspended snow ornaments can be consolation. That consolation can be celebration. That celebration can be silence. That the seasons may fade into each other without warning. And that the thawing can be startling—a red bulb that pops up to alert them: they are not there yet. That she howled at the moon and a song she wasn't prepared to hear rose in response.

respuestas de las madres

after sor juana ines de la cruz

greetings from scorpio's cusp, assuming we ascribe to secular
constellations, forgive us our creole mother tongue, for following our
first light of reason, our young selves, hiding in feathered pages, in
hacienda chapels, in love letters written in lost aztec languages. you say
our sacred villancicos to st. catherine, carry a skeptic slant. we say bless
the good husbands, if we desired them, who wouldn't gift us illegitimate
children, wouldn't gamble away our homes if given the chance. grant us
shelter in books, in latin, in logic, in maps, the physics of this spinning
spherical wonder. consider our penance, written in prophecy, in
persuasion, in piety. if we be too much woman, make us men, amen, that
we may enter into reason rightly. safeguard our salvation. sincerely, in
the name of the mother, the daughter, and the queen of sheba.

lā'aukūkahi

one of us   stayed up
to hear fireworks in rain

our rage   midnight kiss

the question of weather

today, i name
mercurial—paint
a patch of sky

on my thigh, fallen
honeysuckle, sweet
taint, the baby's

wail—wilted vines,
tangled lines, carry
the bouquet with care

over graveled roads
—white noise signals
a familiar storm. i lie

       on my back,
reprieve from heat:
a prism of diffused

light, leave the bags
unpacked, coffee
untouched, longing

for lips no longer
reluctant, basil breaking
earth, remembering

the bouquet i insist on buying
myself from a lonely farm stand
in the country, unmoored
from thin earth-

stained plastic, held
together in my lap, i
plead with you to drive
slower on the gravel roads

the honeysuckle ashes
a pale yellow circle on
my thigh (we 've mapped
the tender places)

while our attentions return
to that rusted coffee can,
the carefully folded three
dollar bills left unattended

on another two-lane coastal road

for roya

salt streaks wind shield
—last time it was rock spit

the semi leaving perfect
circle, fractal, webbed

wet glass: i cannot hold any
thing but this steering

wheel for certain, not even
you, whose name is dream.

if statements

what if the soft spot sinks, the french press we bought for the friends
who never came burns the dark roast on the stove, the skin breaks, or
worse, the rubber, google starts answering our hysteria with a single
smirk emoji, the translation is wrong, the numbers lie, thirty-eight plus
thirteen weeks is not long enough to learn you, it's always already 8 a.m.,
the microbes on the doorknob, the cat's hair, the rodent dust from the
crawl space infiltrate, the blooming magnolias rot the new plank siding,
the yellow caution tape extends past the children's swing set, it rains for
over forty days, four years becomes forever, the epidural is irreversible,
our peeling fingers forget sex, sorry is better than safe, the question is
the only punctuation, provides no room for protection, the water boils
to an empty house?

if i am sorry
promise me your first words are
no apology

[   ]

where does it hurt?

        you arrived parting the red curtain, blood bucketing the sterile
                plastic tarp, abrupt vacancy. neither of us cried.

why did you choose [us]?

        for two days. we were on unfamiliar territory, unsheathing boxes,
    inhaling spores of someone else's divorce, home. we exhaled under
    the leaking roof. there was no cast iron family heirloom to unpack.
    the photo of the woman, your middle name, restrained smile on
                          an already dusty altar.

is this it?

        yes. i remember the unforgiving fluorescence. the floor we circled
    like they commanded, for fear they would turn us back. i lowered
    my head past the nurses' station, the one who smirked *you
    can't handle this*. the midwife who never came.

was it your shame?

                        your name on my tongue, descending...

were you surprised?

everyone, but us.

would you?

for you,

again?

my protection,

with...?

my deliverance,

and what of the secrets?

i tried, i tried, i tried to do it bare, to be fully there. ten cm and swift.
my insides flooded the room, sudden soft belly spilling numb joy,
chapped upturned lips. i smiled at that bitch as she patted my arm.
i swear next time i'll do better, but i can't think about next time
while i'm still crying about this one. today it's snowing and
i'm excited to show you.

her inheritance

*I wish my poems could save us from
our parents' childhoods*
—Sara Borjas

Sooner or later history catches up.
—Erica Hunt

one-half of one-third of the axis of evil
a carcinogenic preference, acquired taste
for plastic, screaming a way thru
—the color blue, broken coral, a
collection of smooth rocks to lay
on an unmarked grave

soft nails that tear at the quick,
hurried step across intersections
to an indifferent greeting: no one
knows how to pronounce your
name

fascination with flame
& glass & sand & tail &
chasing flight, pointer
finger fixed toward the sky
—a thrice-history of fleeing
one-fourth refinanced
one-fourth reverse-mortgaged
one-fourth rented w/ roommate

three-fourths on the spectrum of unemployed
       bill unpaid
under sheafs of red-marked paper, birthed
unto balance owed, decrepit credit score
before even learning to count: ichi, ekahi ...

what to say when a stranger offers candy?
                i say salamat po, mama

catalog of earthly delights

acknowledgement: a gentle
gesture, a soft circling on
your lower back

bread, sliced seeded
with honeyed edges
in an unmade bed

cul-de-sac view
from the new-to-you
cathedral window

drawn shades signaling
the end of another day,
after day, after day

every day

frame of you before her
birth, alongside a lock
of her fine hair, freshly cut

grass, the lawn mower before
a wet weekend, the hard *gah*
against two lonely teeth

heat of his chest in
the almost dark, her
raspberry kisses

in, one—two—three, *out*,
you fall asleep
to each measure

january: chin-to-fleece
cuddles, chimney smoke
you can't scrub out

kitten hair on the counter
sticking to the mismatched
place-setting creases

lavender mist, oiled wrists,
moonstone ring (mama
never wore diamonds)

orb of unplanned pleasure
a parenthetical moment
           remember?

pulsing panties stuffed
in the back of the drawer,
tags intact for a rainy day

query that feels like
a promise and a threat:
who do you think I do this for?

radishes in clean plastic
planters scattered
too close together

sprouting, still morning,
that first sleepy suckling,
sweet orange thumb

takeout eaten with
chopsticks and a side of
90 day fiancé

unearthed cement, sledge
hammer and sage, collapsing
together horizontal

validation, signed, sealed,
delivered by whisper
against your ear

white rabbit candy
with the wrapper that melts
like magic

x the spring, summer
months on the calendar,
count the scrabble scores

you don't admit sometimes,
but you would still choose this
life again, again, again

zenith at forty-two weeks
when she points at the sky
cries *bird* for the first time

hana hou[2]

[2] something that doesn't exist
(i'm looking for the notes)
sweet, repetitive goodbyes my
other selves float between
to allow permission to
capture the fragrance
of blush, undocumented
—my hungry machine,
the continent no one
can find on a map

register arousal

connect the dots on this supple
        skin with your next exhalation
push into this cavern of wet
        longing, dripping paint
brush, lick caked acrylic
        from willing nail beds, blanket
our aching in body fleece, finger
        tip circle lush touch near-full
lips leave breath less
        speaking, more under
standing over, behind, aside
        throw coordinates on the floor
bait whisper misty, pliant,
        soft lifted hood, let lie in re-
membering, slow calling home:

      i'm full

of your fury

cannot contain

these nectarous

sighs, as we un

do

still image of a murmuration

I write to give shape to my death, but also to birds
crossing the sky in slow migrations.
—Lucía Estrada

mistake the bald eagle for a drone. poison the hum-
mingbird with sugar-water solution. there, in the pollen
laden fir, standing tall in the untended backyard,
the woodpecker with a head of auburn unlike anything
you've ever seen.

remember that starling passing over tv highway under
the crossed electrical lines? the flock was swift & efficient,
but the little guy caught up.

look at him go! they land in the wetland past the
intersection; you release your breath.

the bees are out bee-ing while the cat disturbs a nest
of sparrows in the tangle of knobby branches lacing
the connecting fence. black ball of anticipation.

under this jurisdiction, before you learn that no one is
protected, the flock is loud with warning.

famadihana

two shimmies forward & one shuffle back
with arms raised above our heads—an exhumation.

turning of bones. a burning. toaka gasy at
the back of my throat, i stir the pot of charred

rice water over the coals, highland wind whipping
my crossed ankles. something in the singed air re-

calls the season of farmers torching terraced fields.
today, a world away, a coastal forest burns, ashfall

snowflakes i never tongued as a child, nine months
forgotten blood weeping warm down my thigh, my

daughter announcing her first favorite color to us
as a particular shade of lapis lazuli: these mile-

stones surprise. when the rain arrives, we open our
arms, lawn a sea of emerald, dance with the harvest.

kāloakūlua

three musubi, packed
drive toward water   fog, ocean
to glimpse
muddy stars

I : coda

other lives

you scrape gum off
the sidewalk of your
elementary school
for getting caught
with a paper that
reads *penis*, among
other appendages.

you lose something
very specific but
can't remember
what in the backseat
of a dusty red
bronco.

you throw a pizza
box in the street,
which drives the man
you love to leave you.

you are sarah from
fourth grade with
the bangs & the
fucked-up teeth.

you weigh less in
your thirties than
you did as a junior in
high school.

you have holes.
septum, both
nostrils, two lips, a
puncture at the nape
of your neck. you are
reckless with your
skin.

you are hairless in
every way.

your data has not
been backed up in
1153 days.

your hair is
asymmetrical to hide
the cysts on your
cheeks. you never
uncleave the chicken
cutlets from your
chest when fucking.

you only date
drummers in reggae
bands with modest
myspace followings.

you spend your
lunch money on
perms that fall out in
eight hrs or less.

you throw fists at
chicks side-eying
you at the club with
the changing name.

you live in a
bungalow down a
gravel alley off a
major street leading
to a famous beach.

you sleep on a
twin futon, an air
mattress, a trundle
bed, a pull-out
couch, under a
mosquito net, on a
single foam camping
pad, in the middle
of rice fields, on
wooden palettes,
under a tin roof.

you sleep with rats.

you make love in stone castles under the wet skies of jungles in faraway lands.

you sell li hing mui seed door to door, you think SOLICITING means sex. the markup is 250%.

you look up the spelling of chlamydia without autocorrect or a smartphone.

every wed night, you share a hymnal under buzzing fluorescence, lick refrain from each other's lips in the back of the darkened chapel, searching.

you use your cousin's ID to buy rounds of heineken for friends who won't remember you the next day.

you date men who deport someone's father.

you know which couches, dark corners, banana trees in the backyard to avoid at family parties.

your first car is your first love is a rusty navy '86 cabriolet.

you are a charming first date. you tell amusing stories. you know when to smile.

you wake up the night bill clinton flies into hickam air force base, violently. you are too *old* for terrors, for imagining the low-flying jets as the second coming of christ.

your younger brother says, *i remember thinking then, we'd be lucky to make it to our high school graduations.*

there are short
stories about
persian lovers &
ironic finger tattoos
no one will ever read.

you spend your
golden birthday
reapplying mac
matte & taking key
hits with hipster
filmmakers in
bathrooms with
endless mirrors.

you hate flying.

you leave your
friends in harlem in
the flurry of the first
winter snowstorm
to mark the shaft
of some aussie you
matched with on
tinder chanel red.

you fuck a guy
named green who
works in finance,
twice.

you fuck a hot
hollywood-looking
prosecutor who
fucks you into
sobriety.

you fuck a
gentlemanly ginger
in every crevice of
the eighth continent.

you fuck in the
water at kaiona's by
moonlight, return to
his parent's home
in homestead with
sandy toes.

you ask your
grandma if she's
ever been back to
visit. she looks at you
with small, sad eyes.

you pay $700 + the
1.5x deposit for your
first studio in mānoa
valley. 17 & hungry.

you are told that
your hunger is too
much for his god.

once, 20 countries
was a slutty number
to you.

you mistake the
dryer for the
washer, spend years
scraping caked
detergent from the
folds.

postcard from rome

it is a language that takes up
space. pouring out car windows,
steamy, spilling out into wet
streets, occupying whole lanes
with its swagger, a laughter with
out pretense in its articulation
of joy. a song you can hear
playing too loud, too late thru
paper walls, makes you smile in
spite of yourself, tap your toe on
the soft carpet, imagining your feet
are the pair gliding over the linoleum
& your waist the one led in late-night
figurations while the water boils. *bellissima!*

                                          you,
                        in the kitchen corner: amused,
                        tolerated, yet never invited
                        to the table. pretending
                        you don't care about being
                        ignored while you watch
                        everything vigilant, hungry.

is it true that there is no
language that exists among
you? that you'll eat whatever
is left over? that you're a good
girl? who never mews? yet
your pride fills rooms—
walls that don't talk back,
but breathe thinly in
the background. i
recognize your
hollow, how
you long
to be
lion.

origin story

I.   *self-portrait as letter & number*

the hollow of my belly
the hollow of our bedroom
our bedroom reflecting
this new body pleading:
i, not wanting to lose
my definition, the shape
straightening into an upper
case vowel, surprising us both
with its new sound.

II.   self-portrait as cold, beautiful house

that strange triplex with its victorian crown
molding, dancing light, staircase leading
to nowhere   i didn't think i deserved
a kitchen island   my name above
the street named after a sturdy tree   & that tender
gesture   when we signed the lease

                              —before leaving, i woke up
             repeating
a phrase in a language that made sense in my dream:
             phase figure five in the pitch of blue
                                          the key

III.   self-portrait as gloam

i follow the tread
on sand-traced ~~lava~~
~~rock~~ black, release
the shutter, crop
a caravan of lifted
trucks from the frame,
post the caption
home, though
i don't know its
real name, just the
geotag

IV.   self-portrait as mōhalu

        we would listen to willie k
at heʻeia pier in the back of his momʻs van
with the old fishermen & kahaluʻu chronics
& electric eels.
                i used to sneak into his room,
makeshift, built beneath his familyʻs home, stilted
between kalo field & fishpond   in the middle of the night
                that left turn off johnson rd
broke a lot of collarbones.

        once he dreamt i appeared
in the dark at his door & sat
at the foot of his bed, stroking
his sixth toe. he woke up
shivering, door thrown open
to a silver-cast field.

there was that tree his dad
and his dadʻs dad kept cutting down
& then—

        but thatʻs not my story to tell.

V.   self-portrait as morning

                              shelter   nomad
carrying
        itself slow across the slick path:
                              i look for a deviation
                              i run toward the roar
                              i plan my next leap in the water
                    before reaching the shoreline

notes

"a more perfect union (misplaced accent)" loosely translates the Declaration of Independence using only the letters found in the Hawaiian language (5 vowels, 7 consonants) with translations supplied by Nā Puke Wehewehe ʻŌlelo Hawaiʻi then re-translates select words back to English. It was inspired by the work of Sarah DeYoreo.

The title and themes in "act of math" draw from the work of the late Kānaka ʻŌiwi activist and writer Haunani-Kay Trask and the documentary *Act of War—The Overthrow of the Hawaiian Nation* (1993).

"parcel" is an erasure poem inspired by the writing of Layli Long Soldier and uses source text from the City and County of Honolulu's Environmental Assessment for Waimānalo Bay Beach Park (March 2012).

"[   ]" came out of a collaborative project interrogating the birth story, exploring delivery as performance and as conversation and as collaboration between speaker/mother and subject/child. The project was inspired by a lecture on cyborg poetics by Franny Choi (Tin House, Winter 2021) and Bhanu Kapil's *The Vertical Interrogation of Strangers* (2001).

The haiku ("hoku," "māhealani," "lāʻaukūkahi," and "kāloakūlua") are excerpts from an ongoing series tracking moon phases using the Hawaiian lunar calendar. Observations were recorded using the *Hilo ʻIa A Paʻa* journal developed by the Moon Phase Project and Kealopiko.

"still image of a murmuration" is partly an ekphrasis poem after Xavi Bou's ornithographies project (https://xavibou.com/ornithographies/).

The form of "other lives" was inspired by Sara Borjas's poem "We Are Too Big for This House" (2019).

acknowledgments

It takes a village to raise a child, and this book, in many ways, was my firstborn. I am deeply grateful to the community who midwifed its passage into the world.

Thank you to my parents, my brothers, and my entire extended ʻohana for your unconditional love & support. There is no book without you.

Bobak: thank you for laying down to watch the water boil with me. We did it.

Thank you to my USF family: Doug, for the "movable feast" that informed my early MFA journey. And the cohort of incredible writers who read shitty drafts of many of these pieces (*A Poem A Day* peeps, you know who you are).

Thank you to the faculty at PSU: John and Michele, for your generosity and mentorship. And Consuelo, for being family. Katie, Lee, Ann, for facilitating those trips to Sou'wester and for celebrating * every * damn * win.

Thank you to the gracious editors at First Matter Press: ash, Emily, and especially my lead editor, Lauren, for your guidance throughout this whole process. Rae, for your insight & for leaning into our synchronicities. And Lara, for fulfilling my cover collage dreams.

Special thanks to Kristina Marie Darling and Jennifer "JP" Perrine for your generosity & care reviewing this book. I am honored that you would take the time to sit with my work.

Sustainable Arts: thank you for seeing me and for supporting so many parent writers.

Thank you to everyone who believed I had a book in me before I believed it myself: Ms. Jones, Trina, Hope, Regi, Meris, Anu...

I love you, mahalo piha.

Deep gratitude to my Kanaka ʻŌiwi kumu & family, and to the Atfalati, Clatskanie, and Kalapuya on whose occupied lands this manuscript was largely completed

And to the following publications where versions of some poems in the book have appeared: *Frontier Poetry* ("rules of negotiation"), *PRISM international* ("our lady of ʻiolani"), *Ruminate Magazine* ("inherit the wind"), *West Trestle Review* ("if statements"), *Gaze Journal* ("outer-island layover" and "respuestas de las madres"), *The Rumpus* ("parcel"), and *Tupelo Quarterly* ("a more perfect union (misplaced accent)," "act of math," "très passing," "ten-cent flower," and "her inheritance").

CHARITY E. YORO is a steward of words and beings. Since publishing her first broody poem in 8th grade, her writing has appeared in the *New York Times*, *The Rumpus*, *poets.org*, *Tupelo Quarterly*, and elsewhere. Born, raised, and educated on the east side of Oʻahu, she currently lives in Portland, Oregon with her wild, loving family.

FIRSTMATTERPRESS
Portland, Ore.

First Matter Press is a writers' collective in Portland, Oregon, founded in 2018 to dissolve publication barriers for first-time publishing poets and genre-expanding writers. We invite authors into a creative cohort to crystallize manuscripts in dialogue with editors and fellow writers and collaborate with featured artists on original cover art. We are a 501(c)(3) non-profit organization and our authors maintain 100% of book sale proceeds. Please support independent booksellers by shopping for our titles at Bookshop.org

2023
FEATURED COVER ARTIST LARA ROUSE

FLOATING BONES
rae diamond

TEN-CENT FLOWER & OTHER TERRITORIES
charity e. yoro

OUR FAVORITE PEOPLE IN THE ROOM
edited by ash good, lauren paredes & emily moon

2022
FEATURED COVER ARTIST RACHEL MULDER

BETWEEN THESE BORDERS WANDERS A GOLEM
ahuva s. zaslavsky

EVEN THE AIR, TOO HEAVY
riley danvers

ONE ROW AFTER / BIR SIRA SONRA
sonya wohletz

SOMEONE I CAN HOLD GENTLY
xylophone mykland

STORIES FOR WHEN THE WOLVES ARRIVE
hailey spencer

2021

2020

2019

2018

FIRSTMATTERPRESS.ORG